How Does God Choose?

Shiela Y. Harris

How Does God Choose?

Scripture quotations marked KJV are taken from the King James Version of the Bible.

ISBN: 978-09679312-3-4

DEDICATION

This is dedicated to every believer in Christ and those yet to receive Him as their Lord and Savior.

TABLE OF CONTENTS

ACKNOWLEDGMENTS

I wish to acknowledge my aunt and uncle, the late Willie and Vivian
Lykes who always supported me in all of my endeavors,
Pastors Melvin and April Jackson of Grace Unlimited Ministries
(FNA Believers' Christian Fellowship),
Bishop Sheridan & Lady LarLeslie McDaniel, (former
Pastor and First Lady of Worship Center Community Church)
and Pastors Henry and Alicia Pigee'
(of Monrovia Worship Center)
each for their spiritual guidance and influence over the years;
my mother Ruth L. Green my biggest fan,
my brothers and their wives;
James and Thelma Green, Ray and Nazeen Green,
Keith and Gwen Green; my children
Denzil Houston, Kevin Davis (god-son), Chisa Houston and
Damien Houston and finance' De'Andra Simley and
my grand-daughters
Ashley Gene' Smith and Trinity Cummings all for your
continued faithfulness to family and God.

Introduction

If you've read any of my previous books, certainly you would agree they are usually a short read as well as informative and exciting. I believe this to strategically be God's plan for my writing especially when it comes to the things that deal with our spirituality. We arrive to church late and leave early, bible study just does not fit in every believer's busy week and neither does researching or studying. For many, a novel or book filled with romantic whims and sexual connotations will be read in an evening but materials that enlighten us in the things of God we just cannot find the time to read.

God loves us and wants us to succeed. Just as He gave His Son in sacrifice He also touches the hearts of His people through the writing of books and literature that will help the believer get back on track and influence the non-believer to get on board. Though many do, it is not God's desire that His people perish because of a lack of knowledge.

You will find without much filtering but with taste and susceptibility to the Holy Spirit the use of my life's events along with bible principles are incorporated to minister through writing; evoking laughter and tears while enlightening and empowering every reader.

<u>Hosea 4:6</u>

...my people are destroyed from lack of knowledge. "Because you have rejected knowledge, I also reject you as my priests; because you have ignored the law of your God, I also will ignore your children.

When God's people are destroyed and waste away, it isn't because God has lost either His love or strength but moreover because His people lack knowledge. God is not saying that His people are completely ignorant; we have *some* knowledge, but not enough. We probably have just enough to make us think we know it all.

What kind of knowledge do we lack? In the context, the first answer must be we lack *the knowledge of God* (Hosea 4:1). We know God some - perhaps a little - but not *enough.* Of course, some feel they know God well enough already.

The second kind of lacking is the knowledge of God's Word (we have forgotten the law of our God). We know the Word of God some - perhaps a little - but not *enough.* Is it also we think, we also feel we know God's Word well enough already.

It should not surprise us that there is a connection between knowing God and knowing His Word. Some people think that Bible knowledge is boring and much too studious and not necessary for a real walk with God. But God and His Word are extremely connected; interchangeable. Psalm 138:2 says, *You have magnified Your word above all Your name*. When God sought for a term to express His nature, He calls Himself "The Word" (John 1:1).

When we know God for who He really is, it should affect our conduct. When there is no knowledge of God, no conviction of his omnipresence (being present all the time or everywhere at the same time) and omniscience (knowing all things), our <u>secret</u> offences, such as adultery, lying, gossiping and so forth, will prevail. We should not be surprised that continuous sinning leads to continued sin.

My deepest desire as you read what God has given me to share with you, is you gain useable knowledge that will encourage, enlighten, empower, causing positive change and give you clarity as you walk out this Christian journey daily.

The idea for this book as most of my writings comes at some of the most inopportune times. Nestled in my warm bed watching a movie on the Trinity Broadcasting Network (TBN) God gave me this project.

Part of the movies premise was a middle-aged Christian woman and man, lived together unmarried for nine years and were influenced by a new preacher in town to marry. On their wedding day the bride to be has a heart attack and dies. She and the common-law husband married at her bedside in the hospital moments before she passed away.

The preacher responsible for their decision to marry (not their pastor) was in the hospital chapel weeping trying to understand God in the midst of this. The deceased woman's sister entered, sat by the preacher and asked as she sobbed uncontrollable, "How does God choose?" As they both sobbed the preacher looked up solemnly, answering quietly, "I don't know." It was then I realized this was not a question that could be easily answered with comfort in a moment of soluble grief. It also raises the questionable thought, "Could it be answered at all?"

My long awaited evening of rest and relaxation quickly turned into a night of writing. Although tired and in no way interested in working on another book, acting in obedience I realized God was not giving me a choice because my mind was racing with ideas. The thought continued to peak interest and the only way there was going to be sleep for me was to get out of bed, turn on the computer and began typing, recording my thoughts.

Never thought about how God chooses or decides because the thought was always expelled to His sovereignty. To question God seemed to hinge on blasphemy because He is God and that settles it. Right? Recalling scriptures referencing God's authority and power rolled out of my mind.

I also recalled people using the old adage "a flower was plucked by the wayside" meaning when one died they were personally hand-picked by God. Is that it, when we die we are hand-picked? How do we know if purpose and destiny is being fulfilled?

Is purpose being fulfilled and destiny proclaimed when a baby never lives long enough to walk or talk? Was the murder of a young teen used to bring a nation together in their pursuit of justice? What about the parents, his family and friends and how do they find peace in this? Are those protesting following the crowd or are they honestly familiar with the motivation of racial profiling and its injustice?

While understanding God is sovereign there are interruptions in life that will cause speculation and questions to arise and depending on timing we are not going to always be spiritual dealing with some of these events. God loves us so much He sacrificed His ONLY Son Jesus, for us, and yet we often experience tragic and unimaginable events during our lifetime.

How does a man commit murder/suicide and kill himself, his wife and their children? How is it a family drives down a street and their baby in the rear car seat is murdered from a stray bullet? Why do we have so many children and babies suffering and dying so young from disease, neglect and abuse? How does a man take the innocence of a child through the act of molestation or rape? Why do thousands of people perish in earthquakes, floods, tsunamis, tornadoes, hurricanes and other natural disasters?

This and more will be dealt with throughout the pages of this book. Its purpose and focus is to give comfort and clarity, encouragement and understanding as you read, “How Does God Choose?” Enjoy!

Chapter 1
God Is…

The miscarried fetus, the young husband of the bride of two months has a massive heart attack, the teen losing their battle with leukemia, the thirty-seven year old sister loses her fight with Lupus and leaves four small children motherless; how does God decide or choose when our time on earth is up? This question we've all thought but never asked probably because we understand God is sovereign. What does that mean exactly? God is almighty, all-powerful, and unstoppable and does what He wants, when He wants, how He wants to.

In times past our parents always told us not to question God. My thoughts concerning this were always, "Why not?" How will I learn or understand life and its experiences if I cannot question the creator? While relying on their inability to give an acceptable answer, or attempting to understand the mind and ways of God often caused more confusion and frustration.

Why are so many young thriving men being murdered and the addict, gang-banging, good-for-nothing criminal remains to terrorize our communities? I've thought about it many times and will usually dismiss the thought. But there is no better time than now to tackle this head-on, so stay with me because with God's help I am going somewhere with this.

From recent personal experiences I've found the better I understand the character, attributes and sovereignty of God the greater the probability of me accepting what befalls me. During difficult times, whether we are expecting the worse or whether the worse just happens God is never surprised, nor does He panic or regret what has been allowed. Sounds unreasonable, well let's see.

Does God's choosing one over another (if He does such a thing) make Him unrighteous?

Romans 9:14-16

What shall we say then? Is there unrighteousness with God? Certainly not! For He says to Moses, "I will have mercy on whomever I will have mercy, and I will have compassion on whomever I will have compassion." So then it is not of him who wills, nor of him who runs, but of God who shows mercy.

Is there unrighteousness with God? Paul answers this question strongly: Certainly not! God clearly explains His right to give mercy to whomever He pleases in Exodus 33:19.

And the LORD said, "I will cause all my goodness to pass in front of you, and I will proclaim my name, the LORD, in your presence. I will have mercy on whom I will have mercy, and I will have compassion on whom I will have compassion.

I will have mercy on whomever I will have mercy: We first should remember what mercy is. Mercy is *not* getting what we do deserve. God is never *less* than fair with anyone, but fully reserves the right to be *more* than fair with individuals as He chooses.

I am not saying a loss of life or a life changing event should not hurt, surprise us or catch us off our guard. But we put ourselves in a dangerous place when we regard God's mercy towards us as our *right*. If God is indebted to show mercy, then it is not mercy - it is obligation. God's mercy is a benefit of His unconditional love towards us.

Remember this: God's mercy is not given to us because of what we wish to do, or because of what we actually do, but simply out of His desire to show mercy. Remember…God is.

We might find ourselves trying to figure out a balance in life with God as we would with light and dark, good and evil and law and grace. But God Himself is "unbalanced" in this sense, He is entirely good.

Romans 9:18

Therefore He has mercy on whom He wills, and whom He wills He hardens:

God will sometimes glorify Himself through showing mercy; sometimes God will glorify Himself through a man's hardness. This does not mean God persuaded an unwilling, kind-hearted Pharaoh to be hard towards God and His people. In hardening the heart of Pharaoh, God simply allowed his heart to respond the way it actually felt about the matter. Pharaoh had many opportunities to relinquish his pride but he chose rebellion.

Life is like a giant puzzle and we each are assigned various pieces of this giant puzzle. God and He alone know how all the pieces fit together. Let's look back to the beginning as we know it.

Genesis 1:1-3

In the beginning God created the heavens and the earth. Now the earth was formless and empty, darkness was over the surface of the deep, and the Spirit of God was hovering over the waters. And God said, "Let there be light," and there was light.

From the believers point of view we come to the Bible knowing there is a God and He's always been before anything else. The Bible does not make elaborate arguments for the existence of God and neither should we. However, it does tell us how we can know God exists. We know God exist by what we see in creation. People often question where God came from or who made Him but God is the uncreated Being, eternal, and without beginning or end. That's why the aphorism, "Nobody greater or there is none greater" is so powerful.

Genesis shows us the origins of the universe, its order and complexity; the solar system, the atmosphere and hydrosphere, the origin of life, man, marriage, evil, language, government, culture, nations, and religion. It is precisely because people have abandoned the truth of Genesis that society is in such disarray. We must not systematically pick and choose what biblical genre we want to believe but allow God to minister to us through its entirety. If we can without any doubt believe Genesis we really should not have any problem believing the rest of the Bible.

Creation is "spoken" into existence…and God said, "Let there be…" and there was and is. As Christians we understand that the Bible was inspired by God. We study the Word to develop our relationship with God and He reveals to us what is profitable to us as in:

<u>2 Timothy 3:16-17:</u>

All Scripture is given by inspiration of God, and is profitable for doctrine, for reproof, for correction, for instruction in righteousness, that the man of God may be complete, thoroughly equipped for every good work.

God's Word contains no mistakes and is absolutely reliable. Many yet believe the Bible is just a book written by men while others believe it is a book inspired from God. It is both. The Bible is unique in its continuity, circulation, translation, in its survival, honesty, truth and influence because it speaks with one united voice.

It is the most published book ever written, first book to be translated, has survived time through manual transcription, persecution and criticism. In its *honesty*: It deals with the sins and failures of its heroes in a manner quite unknown among ancient literature and had a greater influence on culture and literature than any other book in existence.

Exodus 3:13-14

Then Moses said to God, "Indeed, when I come to the children of Israel and say to them, 'The God of your fathers has sent me to you," and they say to me, 'What is His name?' what shall I say to them?" And God said to Moses, "I AM WHO I AM." And He said, "Thus you shall say to the children of Israel, "I AM has sent me to you."

Moses realized he would need proof before the people of Israel. Before, he thought he had the credentials because he was a prince of Egypt but 40 years of tending sheep took away his sense of self-confidence. Remember not to allow what you do or what you've done in life change who you are in Christ.

Dealing with the text the name **I AM** has within it the idea of *acuity* - that God is completely sovereign and He relies on nothing for life or existence. God doesn't need anybody or anything – He Himself is life.

Also inherent in the idea behind the name **I AM** is the sense that God is "the becoming one" God becomes whatever is lacking in our time of need. The name **I AM** invites us to fill in the blank to meet our need - when we are in darkness, Jesus says *I am the light*; when we are hungry, He says *I am the bread of life*, when we are defenseless, He says *I am the Good Shepherd*, when we are thirsty, He is the living water. God is the becoming one, becoming whatever we need in life.

How does mercy and justice play out in God's choice? If one is suffering with an incurable disease and healing is not the outcome, death would be welcomed. The saved person still wins: no more cares of this world or pain and suffering, but eternal life in a glorified body with Christ.

On the other hand, she was just coming into herself. Great student, loved by all, great things were expected from her and suddenly, without warning, she becomes the unfortunate victim of a homicide during a drive-by because her assailant could not shoot the side of a barn. Merciful...how? There is no justice when the assailant goes free because the weapon cannot be pinned to the crime, or because there is no license plate or concise car description, or some antiquated law is resurrected to save the perpetrator from deserved punishment. Where is the justice? Where is God?

When it is someone else we may have a spiritual grounding but when it directly affects us...we have a different attitude. This attitude has nothing to do with our faith but everything to do with our circumstances that are causing great pain and anguish.

Lest we forget to remember, we each have a divine destiny with God the Father.

Ephesians 1:9-12

Having made known to us the mystery of His will, according to His good pleasure which He purposed in Himself, that in the dispensation of the fullness of the times He might gather together in one all things in Christ, both which are in heaven and which are on earth; in Him. In Him also we have obtained an inheritance, being predestined according to the purpose of Him who works all things according to the counsel of His will that we who first trusted in Christ should be to the praise of His glory.

Part of what belongs to us under the *riches of His grace* is the knowledge of the mystery of His will, God's great plan and purpose which was once hidden but is now revealed to us in Jesus. In the New Testament mysteries are hidden from the heathen but made clear to the believer.

To gather together has the same idea of "to unite" or "to sum up." Paul's idea is that God will make all things "add up" at the end, and right now (believe it or not) He is in the process of coming to that final sum in every person's life.

Though God often uses human instruments to accomplish His plan, we ultimately depend totally upon God both for our resources and accomplishment.

Our God is a God who not only wills; but He works; and He works according to His will. The word *counsel* stands for precise and deliberate planning and arranging, in which the ways and means of carrying out the will are considered and provided for.

It is a must that we remember that God is the GREAT I AM. Our destiny and purpose is excluded from all prediction but it is however, included in His Will.

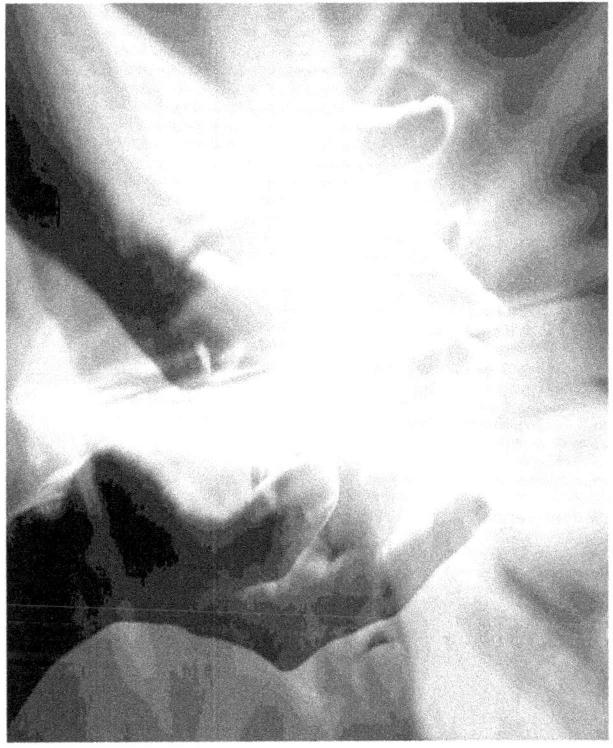

Chapter 2
God's Perfect Will vs. God's Permissive Will

GOD'S PERFECT WILL

When we stand firm on the Word of God, refusing to embrace the ways of the world, having our minds renewed, God allows us to experience His perfect will (or plan) for us as we find in:

Romans 12:2

Do not be conformed to this present world, but be transformed by the renewing of your mind, so that you may test and approve what is the will of God – what is good and well-pleasing and perfect.

Because God is omniscient (all-knowing), He knows what He will accomplish in us. Nothing we do will ever surprise Him because He knows what we will do, and what we would do, in any given situation. Perfect means without error or flaw and God's plans for us will never fail; will never be flawed by some missing piece of information, some unknown detail. God's plan and purpose for each and every believer is for our good, and for His glory. Included in this, as difficult as it may seem, is all the suffering and tragedy that comes to us in life.

2 Corinthians 1:5-5

For just as the sufferings of Christ flow over into our lives, so also through Christ our comfort overflows. If we are distressed, it is for your comfort and salvation; if we are comforted, it is for your comfort, which produces in you patient endurance of the same sufferings we suffer.

Sometimes we think the only resolve will be found in a change of circumstances, but God wants to console us during our difficult times, and to do it through Christ. His perfect will also take into account our ignorance, our fears, our weakness, or sins, and even the sins of others against us.

Everything we ever wanted to ask God about, He knows. The bible speaks of the "will of God" in several different ways, and it is important to understand the differences.

- The "decreed will" of God
  This is God's eternal, preordained plan and purpose, which will not change and cannot be altered. It includes our salvation.

- The "perceptive will" of God
  This is God's will, expressed in the form of principles or precepts given to men. The command not to deceive lets us know it is God's will for us not to deceive others. The command not to steal makes it clear that God's will for us is not to steal. The written Word is an expression of His will. We do not have to pray and ask God about sleeping with someone we are not married to, this is made obvious in His written Word.

- God's "desired will"
  This is concerned with what gives God pleasure, and what does not. We know that God loves to show mercy, and yet He will execute judgment. God's pleasure comes in the salvation of sinners; He does not take pleasure in pouring out His eternal wrath on sinners. When we are confronted with things that are not clear to us as with sin, our choice or desire should be to want to please God and obviously that is the choice that should be made.

- God's "directive will"
  This is God's personal guidance in our lives. It does not violate or conflict with any of the "wills."

❖ <u>The "discerned" will of God</u>
This is our personal perception of God's will for our lives, which comes through wisdom. We gain wisdom through reading God's Word and through prayer. Though many do, Christians should not walk around for years or months, wandering through life, going from church to church, wasting time and life wondering what God's will is for us as individuals.

GOD'S PERMISSIVE WILL

Understanding the will of God aids in our understanding that it is not a *choice* as much as it is **allowed**. The results or outcome, depending on how we are affected is what confuses us and causes us to question God when the upright and innocent suffer. God's permissive will is what He allows, even though it is sin. Examples: God allowed Joseph's brothers to betray him, and to deceive their father, so that He might bring the Israelites to Egypt, where God would spare them, and they would greatly multiply. He allowed the devil to stricken Job with boils but he was not allowed to kill him. God allows man to reject the Gospel, to willfully disobey His laws, to persecute the righteous, and so on. But in all of this, God is still in control, and His purposes are being accomplished. His "decretive will" often allows or permits (His permissive will) men to violate His desired will (what gives Him pleasure) and His prescriptive will (His Word). God's permissive will is never outside His decretive will. God "permits" those things which will lead to the accomplishment of His decretive will.

This is why we sometimes find it difficult to understand some of life's traumatic events because it is all God's perfect plan (the pieces of the puzzle we cannot see). This is the premise of this book, the things we view as "God's choosing." But rather than choice it is more relative to God's will. We must understand that God's plan was formed before the foundation of the world and is manifested and unfolded in time or human history. However, the entire plan was formed from all eternity and it is not subject to change. God is not rustling about trying to work out His plan or make any last minute corrections. When we fumble the ball, or when things go wrong, or when tragedy strikes, according to scripture, God's plan has not erred. He is still on the throne and in control. The tragedy no matter how grim or devastating it may appear, was (or is) a part of God's plan.

God includes our fumbles and allows the tragedies of life in His sovereign purpose. Ultimately and unfortunately, bad things happen to good people.

As severe as crime is today, it is not new or surprising to God. In Genesis 4:4 we find the first recorded murder; Cain kills Able.

Genesis 4:8

Now Cain said to his brother Abel, "Let's go out to the field." And while they were in the field, Cain attacked his brother Abel and killed him.

Parents play an important role in the development of society through the development of our children. Under normal circumstances, most parents want good things for their children. They often wonder if their children are destined for greatness. Adam, and especially Eve, had these expectations for Cain, but it went farther than normal parental hopes and expectations. Adam and Eve expected Cain to be the Messiah God promised and they had seeded and given birth to a murderer.

Hebrews 11:4 makes it plain why the offering of Abel was accepted and the offering of Cain was rejected: *By faith Abel offered up a more excellent sacrifice than Cain.* Cain's offering was the effort of dead religion, while Abel's offering was made in faith, in a desire to worship God in spirit and in truth and God was more concerned with faith in the heart than with artistic beauty of Cain's offering.

Cain became angry because his sacrifice was not accepted. This is comparable to how we react today when someone is favored over, or receives more recognition than another. Our wounded pride leads to anger and if not brought under control we may not physically murder another but we will attack the reputation and character of others with malicious gossip.

God warned Cain that his anger would lead to sin and He gave him a way of escape. Of course, Cain did not heed God's warning and allowed sin to overtake him. There are no gray areas in the bible, if God is not Master over our lives we will ultimately be slaves to sin.

Cain was guilty of committing *premeditated* murder, and therefore clearly ignored God's way of escape. No human had ever died or been killed before, but Cain saw how animals were killed for sacrifice and he took Abel's life in the same way.

The statistics below gives some idea how sin is trying to overtake the world and how widespread crime is against humans.

Random Statistics
United States Crime Rates - 2005-2011

Year	Population	Total	Violent	Murder	Rape	Robbery	Assault
2005	296,507,061	11,565,499	1,390,745	16,740	94,347	417,438	862,220
2006	299,398,484	11,401,511	1,418,043	17,030	92,757	447,403	860,853
2007	301,621,157	11,251,828	1,408,337	16,929	90,427	445,125	855,856
2008	304,374,846	11,160,543	1,392,628	16,442	90,479	443,574	842,134
2009	307,006,550	10,762,956	1,325,896	15,399	89,241	408,742	812,514
2010	308,745,538	10,329,135	1,246,248	14,748	84,767	367,832	778,901

Random: Ethiopia has 75.29 infant mortality rates of 1,000 births. They rank 14 in the world. Main causes are starvation & disease.

These are difficult times for all, but just as sin does not have to overtake us and can be contained, life's events do not have to destroy us.

2 Corinthians 4:8-9

We are hard pressed on every side, but not crushed; perplexed, but not in despair; persecuted, but not abandoned; struck down, but not destroyed.

Paul's life was hard, and it was hard because of his passionate devotion to Jesus Christ and His gospel. Yet, look at the triumph of Jesus in Paul's life: not defeated, not in despair, not discarded and not destroyed. Paul knew the power and victory of Jesus in his life because he was continually in situations where only the power and victory of Jesus could meet his need. We must strive daily to reach this level of strength. This level of strength helps us not to become stagnant or stuck when we are faced with traumatic or negative experiences but moreover we can go through the process that promotes healing and wholeness.

When considering this thought for today, it is easy to see this as just "spiritual things," because some of us live very comfortable lives, and do not suffer much at all. But we should remember that everything Paul says about suffering, he says as a man who has probably suffered more than us, or more than anyone you will ever meet. This was not theory or happenstance to Paul, but real life experience. People who actually experience tragedy may have a more difficult time dealing with or comprehending it. Man will never fully understand the will of God but we must take responsibility for our personal choices and not rely on human wisdom to help us understand or cause us to mistrust God.

The influence of our flesh is powerful and the aid of the Holy Spirit is needed to help us continue depending on God to strengthen our will to align with His will. We must remember that God does not cause sin but sin exists according with His purpose.

God's wisdom and knowledge cannot be comprehended, and His decisions cannot be tracked or predicted. God has consulted no one and no one has advised Him. But because God knows all things He controls and guides all events *for His glory and for our good.* Undoubtedly, this premise is very difficult to comprehend when we are directly affected through a traumatic experience but nevertheless we must trust in Him.

Chapter 3
Bad Things Happen to Good People

Every year, we are bombarded with news reports of horrible events that occur all over the world: serial murderers, mass killings at the hands of terrorist, plane crashes, devastating floods, tornadoes, hurricanes, tsunamis, earthquakes, genocides and on the list goes. There seems to be no end to it. Could all this be in God's plan? God's Word, though puzzling to us, gives us the answer. Look back at:

Ephesians 1:11

In him we were also chosen, having been predestined according to the plan of him who works out everything in conformity with the purpose of his in order that we, who were the first to hope in Christ, might be for the praise of his glory.

God's great plan and purpose which was once hidden is now revealed to us in Jesus. Through the Apostle Paul, and for most it is incomprehensible, God calls us to consider the greatness of God's great plan for the ages and our place in that plan.

Sin is always the product of man's choice, his own negative preference to God. God may permit it, use it, or hinder it, but it is man who chooses to sin in rebellion against God. God did not create man to be a robot but a human with choices created in God's image with the moral responsibility to know God, love God and to obey God. When man is faced with a choice between sin and good he should choose for God. A robot can only do what it is programmed for and this would bring little glory to God; it certainly would not have the capacity for love and true fellowship.

<u>Luke 21:9-11</u>

"But when you hear of wars and commotions, do not be terrified; for these things must come to pass first, but the end will not come immediately." Then He said to them, "Nation will rise against nation, and kingdom against kingdom. And there will be great earthquakes in various places, and famines and epidemics; and there will be fearful sights and great signs from heaven."

If you have paid close attention to catastrophes and disasters over the years we see the Word of God and biblical prophecies being fulfilled. As we live in these difficult times, we should not be frightened by calamities commonly associated with the end times nor lose focus, just know God is in control.

We tend to forget the bible is our guide for our daily life. I do not recommend waiting until tragedy hits to pick up or familiarize yourself with its contents. Moreover, it is important that we pray (communicate with God) and study the Word of God on a regular basis so we can understand and know how to handle life's events. It's not necessary to be a scholar to understand the Word of God. We have many resources available to help us study and the Holy Spirit reveals even the more by opening our understanding.

The teacher/preacher is not responsible for giving us everything we need to absorb from the Word because this would mean most of us would only be exposed one or two days per week (more than likely one). Just as our physical bodies need nurturing with sustenance, our spirit also needs nurturing which through hearing and reading the Word induces spiritual maturation. When we need to recall the Word to encourage us, reading it stores it in our hearts so our minds can recall it.

Even now I dread to think where I would be if it had <u>not</u> been for God's love and some knowledge of His written word. The loss of my father at age 15, pregnant and married at age 16; divorced because of abuse and infidelity by age 18; my eldest brother is drafted and sent to the Viet Nam war (survived) while a neighbor's two sons returned in body bags. There is no way I could've possibly survived life's challenges often with limited finance and disruptions; sudden loss of my husband and other family members without the Word of God. During these and other events the grace of God sustained me. Did I understand and embrace every tragedy? No, of course not!

As events unfold in life we never really know how we will respond no matter how prepared we think we might be. The unexpected tragedies are even more unpredictable and the strongest person may find it difficult and challenging to cope. The more we prepare by reading and applying the Word assures us that God will sustain us and carry us through the healing and recovery process.

Knowing God does not mean we will be exempt from negative experiences. The difference with the believer is in how we face tragedy as opposed to those who do not know God, and is subjected to our continued relationship with God. As believers in Christ, in the worst of times we have access to an inner strength and peace that only His presence can bring.

Surely if tragedy results in death there will be grief but God will take us through the process. If tragedy causes a drastic change in our physical condition or that of a loved one, God will take us through it and use it all for His Glory.

Our justice system gives much to be desired and seems often to favor the criminal. But these laws were established because of unjust practices for the accused and have become loopholes defense attorney's use to get their clients adjudicated of their crime. Though seemingly unfair, much also depends on where the crime is committed and who it is committed against.

Matthew 5:45

In that way, you will be acting as true children of your Father in heaven. For he gives his sunlight to both the evil and the good, and he sends rain on the just and the unjust alike.

By doing this God shows love for his enemies; evil and good. Jesus is teaching us our character as the citizens of His kingdom. We should expect that character to be different from the character seen in the world.

Being able to fall down and get up is good; but it can interfere with our maturation if we are continuously tripping over the same things. Less time is spent developing spiritual maturity while more time is spent stumbling, falling down and getting back up.

I know by now you are probably wondering what happens to the wicked? Why, in some cases are they not prosecuted? How do some remain on the streets or receive minimal punishments that are repeated offenders? Well, let's get back into the Word.

Ecclesiastes 8:12-14

Although a wicked man commits a hundred crimes and still lives a long time, I know that it will go better with God-fearing men, who are reverent before God. Yet because the wicked do not fear God, it will not go well with them, and their days will not lengthen like a shadow. There is something else meaningless that occurs on earth: righteous men who get what the wicked deserve, and wicked men who get what the righteous deserve. This too, I say, is meaningless.

The book of Ecclesiastes, or "the Preacher," is unique in scripture. There is no other book like it, because it is the only book in the Bible that reflects a human, rather than a divine, point of view. This book written by King Solomon is filled with error and yet it is wholly inspired (that's a God *thang*). A statement like this may seem confusing to some because many feel that inspiration is a guarantee of truth; this is not necessarily so. Inspiration merely guarantees accuracy from a particular point of view; if it is God's point of view it is true; if it is man's point of view it may be true, and it may not. If it is the Devil's point of view it may or may not be true, as well, but we need to understand that the Devil's ultimate end, of course, is evil. Inspiration guarantees an accurate reflection of these various points of view.

The text supposes a wicked ruler to do an unjust thing *a hundred times,* and that yet his punishment is deferred, and God's patience towards him *is prolonged,* much beyond what was expected, and the days of his power are lengthened out, so that he continues to oppress; yet he infers that we should not be discouraged. Let me remind you that we will not have answers to everything that God allows but He is still *GOD*...the Great I AM.

As God's people we should certainly be a happy people, though at times we may be oppressed: *"It shall be well with those that fear God,* I say with all those, and those only, *who fear before him.''* It is our character as God's people that we *fear God,* have a reverence of him upon our hearts and make conscience of our duty to him and this because we see his eye always upon us and know it should be our concern to approve ourselves to Him.

When we are at the mercy of proud oppressors we fear God more then they fear Him. It is not necessary for us to quarrel with the wisdom of God, but moreover to submit to it. It is the happiness of *all that fear God,* that in the worst of times *it shall be well with them;* our happiness in God's favor cannot be opinionated, nor should we allow our communion with God to be interrupted by our troubles. In the end we will have a blessed deliverance from and an abundant reward for our troubles. And therefore *"surely I know,* I know it by the promise of God, and the experience of all the saints, *that,* however it goes with others, *it shall go well with them.''* All is well that ends well.

Wicked people are certainly a miserable people; though they prosper, and prevail, for a time, the curse is as sure to them as the blessing is to the righteous: *It shall not be well with the wicked,* as others think it is, who judge by outward appearance, and as they themselves expect it will be; nay, *woe to the wicked; it shall be ill with them* (Isa. 3:10, 11); they shall be reckoned with for all the ill they have done; nothing that befalls them shall be really well for them. N*o event can occur to the wicked which will do them good, rather no event which will not do them harm.*

Do not misunderstand this to mean that all wealthy people are wicked. Not at all. The wicked man's days *are as a shadow,* not only uncertain and declining, as all men's days are, but altogether unprofitable. A good man's days have some substance in them; he lives to a good purpose. A wicked man's days are all *as a shadow,* empty and worthless. These days *shall not be prolonged* to what he promised himself; he *shall not live out half his days,* Ps. 55:23. Though they may be *prolonged* beyond what others expected, yet his day shall come to fall. The greatest fall a human can take is fall short of everlasting life, deeming a long life on earth to be worthless. God's great quarrel with wicked people is for their *not fearing before* him; that is at the bottom of their wickedness, and cuts them off from all happiness.

One dangerous emotion for us to ever have or exercise is to be *angry* with God. I've heard people say they have a problem with God because of a loved one's life being interrupted or someone they care about dearly becomes ill with an incurable and debilitating disease. Oftentimes bad things happen to babies and children, adults and teens the good and bad. To grasp this we really must understand who God is.

Many will ask aloud or think to themselves, "Why did this have to happen with all the good for nothing criminals left walking the streets?" Why this family, or this person, what did they do to deserve this? How often have I quietly thought this or spoken it aloud?

Let's look at Job 38

For years I was under the impression that Job took his fate with a smile on his face. It was not until I began studying for myself that this is far from the truth. Here we find God speaking from amidst a whirlwind. His purpose is to humble Job, and bring him to repent of, and to retract, his passionate inappropriate conversation concerning God's divine dealings with him; and this he does by calling upon Job to compare God's eternity with his own time, God's omniscience with his own ignorance, and God's omnipotence with his own inadequacies.

Job knew nothing about creation; he knew nothing about the production of rain or of the morning light or the darkness of night. He was ignorant of the making of his own soul or how to provide for the animals God created. God was trying to make clear if Job was ignorant concerning the ordinary works of nature how could he pretend to dive into the counsels of God's government and to judge of them?

We must remember when we go about to call God to an account we can expect to be interrogated and called to an account ourselves, that we may be made sensible of our ignorance and arrogance. God here puts Job in mind of what he had said, Job 13:22. *Call thou, and I will answer.* "Now make thy words good.''

Job is very intricate and complex and to avoid a dissertation on the entire book I believe you get the just and that is: no matter how painful our experience we must see God in All His Greatness and trust Him as He orchestrates as the author and giver, the father and fountain, of all wisdom and understanding. One thing is certain and that is we will not understand everything God allows.

3 John 1:2

Dear friend, I pray that you may enjoy good health and that all may go well with you, even as your soul is getting along well.

As I study this text I realized some have wrongly taken this as a guarantee of perpetual wealth and perfect health for the Christian. We should *always* remember although God wants our best and plans only good for us, and often present material prosperity and physical health are part of that good He has for us - and this prosperity and health are absolutely promised as the *ultimate* destiny of all believers. On the other hand, for the present time, God may - according to His all-wise plan use a lack of material prosperity and physical health to promote greater prosperity and health in the scale of eternity.

Nevertheless, *some* people live in poverty and disease simply because they do not seek God's best, follow God's principles, and walk in faith. As well, there are *some others* who say we should use God's general promises of blessing as a way to indulge a carnal desire for ease, comfort, and luxury. So be careful my friends how we use the goodness God bestows upon us.

Surely there will be things we will never know or fully understand. There may be events that are overwhelming and ferociously devastating but God is the *Great* I AM*! Remember, it is dangerous to box with God our arms are much too short and our intellect much too finite.*

Chapter 4
How Much is Enough?

A friend of the family lost her husband and later in life two of her three adult children - one month apart. Another had five miscarriages before she bore two healthy daughters. An acquaintance wants to conceive and give birth to one child while another uses abortion as a method of birth control. Depending on the events of our lives we all at some point may ponder *how much is enough?*

Believers know that the Word of God is encouraging, life changing and edifying and yet we seem to hold tight until tragedy arises. I totally disagree with those who want to attack ones faith because of their reaction towards a tragic event, because ones response does not necessarily have anything to do with their faith. Those who've faced horrific tragedy can identify with this. It would be great to know beforehand how we would react in certain situations, but we can't, we can only speculate and pray for a sustainable sanity and recovery.

There is another old adage that states, "experience is the best teacher" and it truly is. I have experienced embarrassment because of a mate's selfishness and indiscretion; the pain of loss of property, relationship, and loved ones. Though all were painful my reaction to each was surprisingly different and there was definitely a lesson learned from each.

When I am hit hard with adversity and the *"woe is me phase"* passes, I generally ask God, "What is it that you want me to learn from this?" Rather than allowing myself to become angry and bitter I prefer asking God to give me the strength to go through and when the strength is not there I petition Him to please carry me through it. As a believer, no matter the issue the greater questions is, "Why not you?" What makes us feel so wonderful concerning ourselves in the eyes of God that would rouse such a question?

Psalm 56:11

In God have I put my trust: I will not be afraid what man can do unto me.

This is a Psalm David wrote when he heard a mourning dove. We must remember to put our trust in God and not fear what man can do. God is for us! This is so important to remember. Refusing an eternal relationship with God, which Jesus offers us, is worse than any attack a terrorist could bring. Not just in light of eternal life, but there is no relationship which compares to knowing God in this life. He is our purpose in life, our source of comfort, our wisdom in confusing times, our strength and hope. So as confusing as life's events can be we must trust God to see us through them and we must accept His sovereignty.

Jesus said in Mark 14:38:

Watch and pray, lest you enter into temptation. The spirit indeed is willing, but the flesh is weak."

It is not just people recovering from varied addictions or strongholds that battle with their flesh it is an intriguing part of our nature as humans. Theologically, we are trichotomous beings and our nature consists of body, soul and spirit which often wars against itself.

Because of our own ineptness, some of our spiritual battles are often *won* or *lost* before the crisis comes. We knowingly place ourselves in harm's way by traveling the road of destruction. Places we go, people we choose to "kick it" with, things we choose to do and more can be determining factors.

1 Corinthians 10:13

No temptation has seized you except what is common to man. And God is faithful; he will not let you be tempted beyond what you can bear. But when you are tempted, he will also provide a way out so that you can stand up under it.

This guarantees us God's promise to supervise all temptation which comes at us through the world, the flesh or the devil. He promises to limit the temptation according to our capability to endure it – according to our ability as we rely on Him, and not relying on ourselves. The way of escape does not lead us to a place where we escape all temptation (that is heaven alone); the way of escape leads us to the place where we may be able to *bear* it without giving into the temptation.

Some things we experience in life have nothing to do with good or evil but have everything to do with the choices we make. Our choices of unhealthy foods for our daily sustenance, the choice to exercise or not to exercise, uncontrolled eating leads to uncontrolled weight gain and other health problems which leads to debilitating diseases and sometimes an early death. Substance abuse (smoking, drug usage and drinking), are just a few ways we destroy ourselves and our families.

I find it unfortunate some of the things people experience. Some seem to go from one tragedy to another while others have more normalcies in their lives. How much can one person or family take? How do they abstain from bitterness towards life? In our economic state people are experiencing the loss of jobs, homes, health insurance, established credit, dignity, and identity and it often rolls in like a domino effect; one tragedy after the other. Unfortunately this is not something new. From early Bible days to the present we have recorded tragedies:

- Gen 7:4 *Seven days from now I will send rain on the earth for forty days and forty nights, and I will wipe from the face of the earth every living creature I have made."*
- Job loses his entire family and all he owned
- 1928 Atlantic hurricane season – 3,000 fatalities
- 2005 Hurricane Katrina – 1,836 fatalities

- 2011 Mississippi River Flood – 20 fatalities
- 2011 9/11 Twin Towers Terrorist Attack
  3,000 confirmed dead
- In Africa, over 13 million people are affected by famine, drought and war.
- About 30 percent of the men and women who have spent time in war zones experience Posttraumatic Stress Disorder (PTSD). An additional 20 to 25 percent have had partial PTSD at some point in their lives. More than half of all male Vietnam veterans and almost half of all female Vietnam veterans have experienced "clinically serious stress reaction symptoms." PTSD has also been detected among veterans of other wars.

Some of these tragic events were caused at the hand of another and others were an act of nature. What I have deducted from this is ultimately, no matter how devastating the tragedy or the unfortunate events in life, God is still in control and is fully aware of everything that happens. Life may take us by surprise but nothing ever surprises God.

Chapter 5
Binding and Loosing

Matthew 16:19

"And I will give you the keys of the kingdom of heaven, and whatever you bind on earth will be bound in heaven, and whatever you loose on earth will be loosed in heaven."

The idea here is not that Peter will admit people to heaven, but that Peter opened the door of the kingdom to both the Jews and the Gentiles.

Matthew 18:18

"I tell you the truth, whatever you bind on earth will be bound in heaven, and whatever you loose on earth will be loosed in heaven."

If one among the church is adamantly unrepentant, they are to be removed from fellowship.

In this verse, Jesus is speaking directly to the apostle Peter and indirectly to the other apostles. Jesus' words meant that Peter would have the right to enter the kingdom himself, which he would have general authority symbolized by the possession of the keys, and that preaching the gospel would be the means of opening the kingdom of heaven to all believers and shutting it against unbelievers. Jesus promises that Peter - and the other apostles - would be able to set the boundaries authoritatively for the New Covenant community. This was the authority given to the *apostles and prophets* to build a *foundation* but we should exercise the power of binding and loosing that Christ gave to His Church.

Ministers act according with the authority of binding and loosing when they preach pardon and peace to the repented, wrath and the curse to the non-repented, in Christ's name.

Peter and the other disciples were to continue Christ's work on earth in preaching the gospel and declaring God's will to men, and they were armed with the same authority as He possessed. In Matthew 18:18; there is also a definite reference to the binding and loosing in the context of church discipline. The apostles do not assume Christ's lordship and authority over individual believers and their eternal destiny, but they do exercise the authority to discipline and, if necessary, excommunicate disobedient church members.

Binding is like a temporary spiritual handcuffing. We can bind a demon spirit, like restraining with rope or chains. On the other-hand we cannot bind a person's freewill but we can bind the demons that are influencing a person. Binding on earth refers to our physical location; right now, on earth. Jesus is saying that the authority to bind and loose are provided for us right here on earth.

The word "heaven" in Greek is referring to air but not the heaven we go to when we die. It is referring to a realm. The bible states in Ephesians 2:6 we are seated in the heavenly realm with Christ. We were below the angels and demons, but as believers we are now seated above the angelic realm and seated with Christ. So here the word heaven is referring to the spiritual realm; the air, where the spirits dwell and operate. In Ephesians 2:1-2, Satan is known as the "prince of power of the air."

<u>Ephesians 2:1-2</u>

As for you, you were dead in your transgressions and sins, in which you used to live when you followed the ways of this world and of the ruler of the kingdom of the air, the spirit who is now at work in those who are disobedient.

Therefore when we bind something here on earth it will be bound in a spiritual realm as well. Additionally, we also refer to loosing as releasing good things into people's life such as blessings or God's love.

But God's love is not bound so there is no need to loose it. But there is a reference in Luke 13:12 of Jesus loosing a captive; "*and when Jesus saw her, He called her to Him, and said unto her, Woman thou art loosed from thou infirmities.*"

It is a power to *bind and loose,* that is (following the metaphor of the keys), to shut and open. The keys to the Kingdom are:

The Key of *Doctrine*
Called the key of *knowledge.* This is an ordinary power hereby conveyed to all ministers, to preach the gospel as appointed officers; to tell people, in Jesus' name, and according to the scriptures, *what is good, and what the Lord requires of them:* and they who *declare the whole counsel of God,* should use these keys well void of manipulation and gimmicks.

The Key of *Discipline*
Christ's ministers have a power to admit into the institutional church; *"Go, disciple all nations, baptizing them;* those who profess faith in Christ, and obedience to him, admit them and their seed members of the church.''

We must be carcful in how we knowing allow sin and wickedness to operate without reproach in the church. This is not just inclusive of parishioners but pastors and leaders as well. Unbridled sin breeds sin. Of course we must established godly ways and use wisdom but to ignore sin is dangerous.

Pastors have a power to expel and cast out such as have lost their church-membership, that is binding; refusing to unbelievers the application of gospel promises and the seals of them; and declaring to such as appear to be wounded by *bitterness and bond in sin,* as Peter did to Simon Magus, though he had been baptized; and this is a binding over to the judgment of God.

They have a power to restore and to receive in again, upon their repentance, such as had been thrown out; to loose those whom they had bound; declaring to them, that, if their repentance be sincere, the promise of pardon belongs to them. This is a method used by pastors who find it necessary to discipline leaders; they release them from their duties and have them to sit for a season.

To bind on earth refers to our physical location; right now, you are on earth. Jesus is saying that the authority to bind and loose are provided for us to use right here on earth.

"I tell you the truth, whatever you bind on earth will be bound in heaven, and whatever you loose on earth will be loosed in heaven."

Chapter 6
Pure Evil

As usual, when I awaken any given morning I pray and then the remote is clicked to turn on the television to view the news, weather, traffic, etc. Much to my amazement there was breaking news regarding a massacre in a movie theater in Aurora, Colorado. It was the midnight showing of the new action packed super-hero movie, "The Dark Knight Rises." Expected to be one of the highest grossing movies for the year, movie buffs often dress in character costumes for the opening showings and stand in line with others for hours. This is not a refute for this or any other movie because I definitely have plans to see it. But the timing is so apropos when trying to describe the essence of *pure evil.*

At the exact moment (within the first twenty-minutes) of an explosive shooting scene in the film, a gunman enters the theater throwing tear gas canisters and firing upon the people. For a second, some thought it was all part of the movie's opening but they began to see people falling, laying in blood, running covered in blood, screaming in panic.

Listening and watching overwhelmed me; not since 911 has anything affected me like this, my spirit man was heavily grieved. Went about my routine for the day but nonetheless stunned and the thought of the breaking news story saddened me to the point of texting friends asking for prayer. Some misunderstood my request, thinking I was fearful because of the tragedy. My emotions were due to an overpowering empathy for all involved and affected, because this senseless act caused a meaningless loss of innocent lives and injuries; the youngest a four-month old baby wounded and a six-year old girl died.

Americans are not immune to attacks or massacres we've survived the terrorists attacks of 911 (2001); Columbine High School Massacre 1999 - 15 died / 24 injured Eric Harris and Dylan Klebold were the gunmen; University of Texas Clock Tower Shooting 1966 - 18 killed / 31 injured / Charles Whitman gunman; Virginia Tech Massacre 2007 - 32 killed, many more injured / Seung-Hui Cho gunman; Red Lake High School Massacre 2005 - 10 killed / 12 injured / Jeff Weise gunman.

As I pen this, I realize this chapter is being added because God wanted me to share my emotional encounter of this unfortunate event. Inasmuch as my flesh was rebelling because I did not want to deal with this but acting out of obedience the addition of this chapter began, and my spirit calmed and peace begin settling within.

Before this tragedy occurred and as advertisement was pouring out in the media leading up to the first showing, the movie's villain was described by Sam Rueben, Channel 5 news entertainment anchor, as the *embodiment of pure evil; terrorist and anarchist.* This description stood out and stuck with me for the entire week, leading up to the massacre and on the day of the massacre he again described the villain as such.

How do we even begin to understand the nature of such tragedies? *Pure evil* can include those with no proper home environment to raise consciousness, or those with brains so far variant from most that there is no impulse control and other mid-brain structures which influence emotion and other behavioral capacities. *Pure evil* is when one does wrong to other people, and know it's wrong, and are proud of the wrong, and reward themselves for the wrong. A person of this nature voids negotiations because they are impermeable to normal emotions.

This is the instruction in 1 Peter 5:8-9. *Stay alert! Watch out for your great enemy, the devil. He prowls around like a roaring lion, looking for someone to devour. Stand firm against him, and be strong in your faith.* Remember that your Christian brothers and sisters all over the world are going through the same kind of suffering you are. We must remain clear-headed (sober) and watchful (vigilant), because Satan has not yet been bound and restrained for 1,000 years as Revelation 20:1-2 says he will be and at the present time, the devil walks about. But we are empowered to resist the devil. Though we can hear his roar and sense his deception we can resist.

John 10:7-10 reads: *Then Jesus said to them again, "Most assuredly, I say to you, I am the door of the sheep. All who ever came before Me are thieves and robbers, but the sheep did not hear them. I am the door. If anyone enters by Me, he will be saved, and will go in and out and find pasture. The thief comes only to steal and kill and destroy; I have come that they may have life, and have it to the full.*

Surely you realize just from this text the enemy's job is to cause mass destruction in the worse possible way. There is also reference in the scripture to a different type of sheepfold, one used out in the fields, not in the towns. A "field" sheep pen was an enclosure for sheep with only one entrance. It might be a cave, a stone or mud-brick structure, and it might or might not have a roof. In a "field" sheepfold, the shepherd actually laid his body across the entrance, to keep the sheep in and to keep out the wolves. The shepherd was in fact the door. *Thief* implies deception and trickery; *robber* implies violence and destruction. These take away life but Jesus gives life and He gives it abundantly. Regardless of the shepherds protection the thief, the enemy still captures and kills sheep.

This kind of evil is impenetrable to negotiations and emptied of empathy and emotion. Their joy and excitement would be to arouse and tap into our greatest fears and horrors. We must remember that evil exists in its purest and worse form and moreover, God is a gentleman and will not force us to change but on the contrary, we must invite Him in.

When the lives of persons that cause such death and destruction are reviewed and investigated the quintessence of their propensity of *pure evil* is there…but no one sees it. They are usually quiet, strange, secluded, unassuming individuals who do not feel comfortable with the norms of life. As they continue in their world of darkness it grows dimmer until the evil implodes them into action. The prince of darkness, the enemy, the devil is real and his characteristics do not change but moreover intensify with time.

A devil type being appears in many cultures. It is usually a representation of evil, sin or temptation. People who do not subscribe to a religious belief dismiss claims that such a being exists. The devil is believed in many religions and cultures to be a powerful, supernatural entity that is the personification of evil and the enemy of God and humankind. The bible list him as worthless, the enemy, represented as a serpent, a tempter, ruler of demons, god of this world, a liar and the father of lies, adversary, angle of the bottomless pit, destroyer, the wicked one and accuser of the brethren. Undoubtedly, he is an awful entity and we have no reason to fear him but we must beware of how he is introduced in the elements of our daily lives including our entertainment. He is not to be purposely reckoned with or his wicked and evil character taken lightly.

Stephen King is my favorite secular writer and I am a fan of science fiction. However, as I age and as technology and special effects become more realistic, I am finding to sleep comfortably what I choose to view on television, at the movies and in other media have to be reconsidered. For me, oftentimes reading the book is easier and less stressful than viewing the movie (although I still view action movies that I sometimes regret later.)

It's safe to surmise if we are to glean anything from this chapter God wants us to remember as we are entertained through media, books, films, games and so on, evil's personification is ever present. There will be people who somehow lose the ability to differentiate between entertainment and reality. Unfortunately, the psychopathic and psychotic are a part of this world and will be until the end of time. We cannot blame the film industry no more than we could blame any author for someone's personality disorder marked by aggressive, violent, antisocial thoughts and behavior and a lack of remorse or empathy.

As horrific as this massacre was one victim stated they believe they heard the automatic assault rifle jam and the gunmen resumed shooting with handguns. During the seconds that the assault rifle jammed some were able to escape. Had it not jammed, the death toll would be even more massive.

One thing is certain, we should not walk in fear but be wise and know that life is a precious commodity and all our days are numbered. Although *Pure Evil* and its satanic and sadistic influences causes people to carry out the most unthinkable or unimaginable act we must realize it will always be present until we go home to glory. But also remember that *God is* greater.

Chapter 7
Who's in Charge?

Genesis 1:26

Then God said, "Let us make man in our image, in our likeness, and let them rule over the fish of the sea and the birds of the air, over the livestock, over all the earth, and over all the creatures that move along the ground."

To understand our responsibility in all this we must return again to the beginning. The Hebrew word for dominion is a verb "radah" and it means to subjugate or have rule over or responsibility for. Over time the earth has become over populated, its land overused, desolating our rain forest and killing ourselves with food preservatives and additives. In addition, much of our fish and wild life's natural habitat is being destroyed.

Around 40% to75% of all biotic species is indigenous to the rainforests. It has been estimated that there may be many millions of species of plants, insects and microorganisms still undiscovered in tropical rainforests. Tropical rainforests have been called the "jewels of the earth" and the "world's largest pharmacy", because over one quarter of natural medicines have been discovered there. Rainforests are also responsible for 28% of the world's oxygen turnover, processing it through photosynthesis from carbon dioxide and consuming it through respiration.

Tropical and temperate rainforests have been subjected to heavy logging and agricultural clearance throughout the 20th century and the area covered by rainforests around the world is shrinking. Biologists have estimated that large numbers of species are being driven to extinction (possibly more than 50,000 a year; at that rate, says E. O. Wilson of Harvard University, a quarter or more of all species on Earth could be exterminated within 50 years) due to the removal of habitat with destruction of the rainforests.

The forests are being destroyed at a rapid pace. Almost 90% of West Africa's rainforest has been destroyed. Since the arrival of humans 2000 years ago, Madagascar has lost two thirds of its original rainforest. At present rates, tropical rainforests in Indonesia would be logged out in 10 years and Papua New Guinea in 13 to 16 years.

At some point man has to take responsibility for deforestation and the affects it is having on human survival and will continue to have in the future if we do not conserve what we have left.

The industrial age brought with it factories with enormous automated machinery and faster transportation. The Industrial Revolution was a period from 1750 to 1850 where changes in agriculture, manufacturing, mining, transportation, and technology had a profound effect on the social, economic and cultural conditions of the times. It began in the United Kingdom, and then subsequently spread throughout Western Europe, North America, Japan, and eventually the rest of the world.

Our responsibility was and is to take care of God's creation but science and technology has evolved so swiftly the balance of nature and life in general has fallen out of sync. Consequently, our air and water is polluted, our food is over processed and pumped with chemicals that throw off the balance and development of animals and the human body and plant cells. Now we are battling with and threatened by incurable diseases, untreatable bacteria, contaminated foods, pandemics and super flu's.

How about, "world hunger?" God gave us distinctive instructions in the beginning. With His infinite wisdom God knew there would always be poor people but we are to give to the poor and needy in our land and not just around holidays but as long as the need present itself. If every nation stopped looking to the other to solve hunger entire nations of people would not die. One economist said if everyone in the world gave one dollar towards hunger, people would not be starving.

Deuteronomy 15:11

There will always be poor people in the land. Therefore I command you to be openhanded toward your brothers and toward the poor and needy in your land.

Each city, county, state and country has the ability to minister to the less fortunate around them by giving. Somehow over the year's greed and self-preservation subdued us and the best we can offer is pity as we look the other way. We destroy farmland and vital echo systems for housing and huge corporate projects as each generation leaves the problem to the next.

Our echo systems have been further destroyed by the excessive hunting of animals, fishing irresponsibly, tilling our farmlands carelessly, oil spills and the building of dams and other projects. Plants and animal species are becoming extinct because of our gross negligence.

The governments on all levels discuss the problems, have summits and establish plans that often do not ever get off the table and people are dying needlessly from hunger and lack of simple medical care. The greatest mistake we've made as a nation and as a people created in God's image and established on the principles of the Word of God is we now have removed God from almost everything except the church (and that is debatable). We sit back and talk about how wrong it is to remove prayer from schools, civic meetings, our currency, and Christian holiday displays, and that's it. We talk while others who are not citizens demand equal rights in a country they care nothing about.

In the first chapter we discussed how the book of Genesis shows us the origins of the universe, order and complexity, the solar system, the atmosphere and hydrosphere, the origin of life, man, marriage, evil, language, government, culture, nations, and religion. It is precisely because people have abandoned the truth of Genesis that society is in such disarray.

We continue functioning as though it's all good while the very complex entities that make up our universe are being destroyed. The ozone layer, Chlorofluorocarbons (CFCs) and other halogens (all man-made gases) emitted from industry rise to the stratosphere where ultraviolet radiation breaks them up and releases their chlorine. Chlorine destroys the ozone layer. Decreasing ozone means increases in melanoma (skin cancer), cataracts, famine (loss of arable land, and damage to crops). This would only occur in areas that had this thinning or hole in the ozone.

Earth's surface receives more Ultra-Violet-B, as ozone is the only gas currently in our atmosphere that absorbs Ultra-Violet-B. Ultra-Violet-B is also absorbed by soil, metered depths of water, and directly by the Deoxyribonucleic Acid (DNA) of all surface life. DNA absorbing Ultra-Violet-B ends up increasing rates of cancer, mutation, and decreases crop yields. Ultra-Violet-B also causes cataracts to form in eye structures in animals (including Man).

We are self-destructing slowly, but surely

We do not lend enough time for long-term testing to discover all the possible pros and cons, especially the cause and effect of medicine and products in comparison to human life and environment.

God left an operation manual to be used for all time in caring for His magnificent creation. Unfortunately, we do what's convenient and in sublime ignorance compete with God: cloning, organ transplanting, hybrid-plants and experimentation that has us bordering blasphemy. Scientific discoveries are great except when we overstep our moral obligation to God and mankind. It is during this time we are bound to experience unfavorable consequences of climatic changes such as global warming, lack of sufficient seasons of rain in some areas and flooding in others and extended seasons of extreme cold.

Though God is all powerful, all knowing and everywhere at the same time we cannot expect Him to resolve something that we can prevent or fix ourselves. We must take responsibility for how we have abused this place called earth. Whether we take responsibility or fight to stop its misuse one thing is certain, we will continue suffering the consequences of our choices.

Synopsis

The title of the book was chosen to peak interest because to be politically, scripturally or theologically correct God does not choose our outcome and moreover, it is based on His predestined Will. We were created free moral agents, given guidelines and instructions in the bible and then left to make choices.

Know this: We will never thoroughly understand God.

As believers we are not under the world's financial system although we feel the effects of our downward spiraling economy. We know in the natural the quality of life is plunging while the cost of living is soaring.

Many have experienced the loss of employment, homes, accrued debt (limited income) and threatened job security. In spite of the economic crunch some have continued paying tithes and giving offerings. But with that we often fail to realize God as our source of resources, our Jehovah Jireh and not our increase from employment or retirement, social security, welfare, alimony, general relief (GR) or child support.

God is not above allowing things to happen to bring back to our memory He is our real source. We must stop giving Him our problems and then retrieving them for the purpose of trying to help Him solve them. Seriously, God does not need our help in problem solving.

Romans 1:18-23

Why the human race is guilty before God: demonstrations of our ungodliness and unrighteousness.

Against all ungodliness and unrighteousness of men, who suppress the truth in unrighteousness, because what may be known of God is manifest in them, for God has shown it to them. For since the creation of the world His invisible attributes are clearly seen, being understood by the things that are made, even His eternal power and Godhead, so that they are without excuse, because, although they knew God, they did not glorify Him as God, nor were thankful, but became futile in their thoughts, and their foolish hearts were darkened. Professing to be wise, they became fools, and changed the glory of the incorruptible God into an image made like corruptible man; and birds and four-footed animals and creeping things.

Ungodliness refers to man's offenses against God; unrighteousness to the sins of man against man. Mankind does in fact suppress the truth of God. Every truth revealed to man by God has been fought against, disregarded, and deliberately obscured.

His invisible attributes are clearly seen: God has shown us something of His eternal power and divine nature through creation, by the things that are made. He has given a *general revelation* of our inherent responsibility that is obvious both in creation and within the mind and heart of man.

The universal character of this revelation and the clarity of it leave man without excuse for rejecting it. Lenski says, "Men cannot charge God with hiding himself from them and thus excuse their irreligion and their immorality."

We are terribly mistaken if we think that it is God's *mercy* or *kindness* that allows man to continue in sin. On the contrary it does imply our overt disregard for His loving kindness through grace and mercy. It is actually His *wrath* that allows us to go on destroying ourselves with sin. It is also a sin for us to misuse God's mercy (what we do not deserve) to receive continuous forgiveness. That is not showing God love but moreover it's a slap in God's face.

Man's disobedience can at times be compared with the heathen; one who does not believe in an established religion; pagan; one who does not acknowledge God. The difference is as a nation we believe in

God but we do not obey Him or acknowledge His Word in our daily lives.

THE DIFFERENCE AND DISTANCE BETWEEN GOD AND MAN

Isaiah 53:8

"For My thoughts are not your thoughts, nor are your ways My ways," says the LORD. "For as the heavens are higher than the earth, so are My ways higher than your ways, and My thoughts than your thoughts."

God doesn't *think* the way we do. We get into a lot of trouble when we expect that He should think as we do. Because we are made in the image of God, we can relate to God's thoughts, but we cannot master them.

There are going to be many times we will not understand why God does the things He does or allows certain things to happen. But the difference between our ways and thoughts and God's is that He knows the end from the beginning. Therefore, He does not have to wonder whether what He has allowed or has done is right.

Nor are your ways My ways: God doesn't act the way we do. He does things His way, and His ways are often not our ways. We get into a lot of trouble when we expect that God should act the way we do.

The distance will never be closed; God will always be God, and we will always be human. But when our salvation is complete, and we are united with the LORD in glory, the distance will be as close as is possible.

Matthew 13:10-12

The disciples came to him and asked, "Why do you speak to the people in parables?" He answered and said unto them, Because it is given unto you to know the mysteries of the kingdom of heaven, but to them it is not given.

Mysteries are hidden secrets (not known to everyone). God's dealings with us are determined by our knowledge of Him. Example: We cannot believe in healing if we do not know God as a healer.

We must learn in this life to truly trust God, especially in difficult situations, traumatic experiences and during times of great losses.

**TO GET WHAT GOD HAS
WE HAVE TO DO WHAT GOD SAYS (TODD COONTZ)**

Lastly, to answer the question used as the title for this book, "How Does God Choose," He doesn't, we do. We choose or reject (there is no gray area) according to how we respond to His Word and accept His will. Although we live in a world with evil just remember God will always provide a way through His Word to live in peace and hope.

For this is what the LORD says– he who created the heavens, he is God; he who fashioned and made the earth, he founded it; he did not create it to be empty, but formed it to be inhabited– he says: "I am the LORD, and there is no other.

Isaiah 45:18 (NIV)

Bibliography

Ask.com

Atmospheric Sciences. Answers.com

Deffenbaugh, Bob. Bible.org. Wisdom & Will of God.

Disastercenter.com/crime/uscrime.htm

Great Bible Study.com

Guzik, David. "Study Guide for Genesis." Enduring Word. Blue Letter Bible. 7 Jul 2006. 2012.

Guzik, David. "Study Guide for Exodus." Enduring Word. Blue Letter Bible. 7 Jul 2006. 2012.

Guzik, David. "Study Guide for Deuteronomy." Enduring Word. Blue Letter Bible. 7 Jul 2006. 2012

Guzik, David. "Study Guide for Hosea. " Enduring Word. Blue Letter Bible. 7 Jul 2006. 2012.

Guzik, David. "Study Guide for Isaiah." Enduring Word. Blue Letter Bible. 7 Jul 2006.

Guzik, David. "Study Guide for Mark." Enduring Word. Blue Letter Bible. 7 Jul 2006. 2012.

Guzik, David. “Study Guide for Matthew.” Enduring Word BlueLetterBible. 7 July 2006.2012

Guzik, David. "Study Guide for Luke 21." Enduring Word. Blue Letter Bible. 7 Jul 2006. 2012.

Guzik, David. "Study Guide for John." Enduring Word. Blue Letter Bible. 7 Jul 2006. 2012.

Guzik, David. "Study Guide for 1 Peter." Enduring Word. Blue Letter Bible. 7 Jul 2006. 2012.

Guzik, David. "Study Guide for Romans." Enduring Word. Blue Letter Bible. 7 Jul 2006. 2012.

Guzik, David. "Study Guide for 2 Timothy." Enduring Word. Blue Letter Bible. 7 Jul 2006. 2012.

Henry, Matthew. "Commentary on Job." Blue Letter Bible. 1 Mar 1996.

Henry, Matthew. "Commentary on Ecclesiastes." Blue Letter Bible. 1 Mar 1996.

Henry, Matthew. "Commentary on Psalms." Blue Letter Bible. 1 Mar 1996. 2012.

National Center for Post-Traumatic Stress Disorder (PTSD) http://www.ptsd.va.gov/about/index.asp

Pocket Dictionary. Theological Terms 1999. Stanly J. Grenz, David Guretzki, Cherith Fee Nordling

Smith, Chuck. "Study Guide for Ephesians." The Word For Today. Blue Letter Bible. 1 Mar 1996. 2012.

Smith, Chuck. "Study Guide for 1 Corinthians." The Word For Today. Blue Letter Bible. 1 Mar 1996.

Smith, Chuck. "Study Guide for 2 Corinthians." The Word For Today. Blue Letter Bible. 1 Mar 1996.

Wikipedia.org. “Devil”

Wikipedia.org. “The Industrial Revolution”

Wikipedia.org. “The Tropical Rain Forrest”

Walker, W. L. "Consume", *International Standard Bible*

Encyclopedia. Edited by James Orr. Blue Letter Bible. 1913. 5 May 2003

World Fact Book, The CIA. Library publications Online.

Wycliffe Dictionary of Theology. 1999. Everett F. Harrison, Geoffrey W. Bromiley, Carl F. Henry (Editors)

Yahoo.com – What is Pure Evil.

About the Author:

Shiela Y. Harris

Ms. Harris is an anointed, multitalented woman, songwriter, and motivational-speaker, ordained elder, preacher of the Gospel, life coach, poet and author and has a strong deliverance ministry for women. One of her first teachings, "How to be Free from Excess Baggage," became her first publication. During week-end summits; from clergy to lay-persons, many have received total deliverance from excess baggage.

She also serves as a volunteer writer for an Antelope Valley Community Newspaper, "Antelope Valley Sentinel," teaches bible study at the Intercommunity Care center and Long Beach Rescue Mission – Lydia House for women. Her latest venture in ministry is partnering with Springs of Hope Grief Care Center with pastor Juanita Matthews in Long Beach, California, a non-profit organization that supports through group grief-guidance, the very difficult season which accompanies death and loss of a loved one, divorce, job loss, other major losses, and sudden life changes.

As a teen mother she completed her secular education while working full-time for the County of Los Angeles, a mother of three children and very active in ministry. Shiela received her BA from California State University, Dominguez Hills (Cum Laude) and to further equip her for ministry she attended the Southern California School of Ministry (First Church of God Inglewood Campus) receiving a Masters in Ministry (Cum Laude) and was one of the commencement ceremony speakers.

She and her late husband, Pastor Ted Harris served as Executive Pastors for Grace Unlimited Ministries under Pastors Melvin & April Jackson and Church of the Word Ministries, South Bay under Pastors Henry & Alicia Pigee' totaling over 15 years. Amongst her many duties she also volunteered as editor for the church monthly newsletters. She currently is a member of Worship Center Community Church, Long Beach, California under Pastor Russell Lewis and First Lady Keisha Lewis (former Pastor Sheridan McDaniel is the presiding Bishop).

As she tackles and dedicates her life to the task God has set before her, ministering to women helping them reach a place of divine wholeness and wellness in God, it is through her personal experiences coupled with biblical principles that many of her teachings developed. People want and need truths. For this and other reasons, she is transparent as she uses life's mistakes and accomplishments to encourage and inform, and to empower and equip.

Ms. Harris is well versed in many areas and some of her teachings are: "Surviving the Loss of a Loved One," "Ministering to Your Pastor," Signs of an Abusive Relationship and How to Get Out," "Waiting on God - For Your Mate," "Church Administration & Staff Training," to name a few. Other publications can be found on createspace.com: "Surviving the Loss if a Loved One," "Ladies No More Fishing," and "How to Be Free from Excess Baggage."

In conclusion, the greatest of her many passions are writing books to motivate and help others, writing poetry and teaching. Her favorite scripture is Proverbs 3:5-6 "Trust in the Lord with all your heart and lean not on your own understanding; in all your ways acknowledge him, and he will make your paths straight." (NIV)

OTHER BOOKS:

How to Be Free From
Excess Baggage
https://www.createspace.com/3775215

Ladies No More Fishing
https://www.createspace.com/3750467

Surviving the Loss of a Loved One
https://www.createspace.com/3740274

www.ingramcontent.com/pod-product-compliance
Lightning Source LLC
Chambersburg PA
CBHW060427090426
42734CB00011B/2478

* 9 7 8 0 9 6 7 9 3 1 2 3 4 *